Coarse Fishing

by Peter Collins and
Colin Graham
Drawings by Jimmy Randell

produced in collaboration with the
NATIONAL FEDERATION OF ANGLERS

CONTENTS

INTRODUCTION

Too many newcomers to angling seem to think that fishing is easy. It looks easy when you know precisely what to do, but the art of catching fish has to be learned. Many beginners quickly become disillusioned and lose interest, eventually deciding that fishing was not really for them after all. This is unfortunate for angling can become an absorbing and worthwhile recreation for those prepared to learn its finer points. Then it can be great fun. It's always best to begin with the help of someone who is already an angler. If you are not fortunate to have such a friend, this book sets out to bridge that gap in a way which, we hope, will convince you that coarse fishing can become easy once you have absorbed the basics. Coarse fishing is like life . . . you've got to learn to walk before you can run. Dream of monsters in your net by all means, but don't expect to catch them at the start. Aim to catch any fish that are available to you . . . even small ones. In your early days, there'll be lessons to learn with every fish you catch.

It could be argued that it is not now so easy to catch fish as in the past. There are fewer fish and these are keenly sought by ever increasing numbers of anglers. Fish *have* become harder to catch. On the credit side, the tackle used to catch fish has improved out of all recognition in the last 20 years. It is still improving. This has helped to offset the problems just mentioned. Just how these improvements help you is something we'll be making clearer later.

Suffice to say for the moment that when you go fishing with confidence, backed by a degree of ability, you will usually be seeking a particular species of fish. As an absolute beginner, you may find this hard to understand, but later you will realise why

this should be so. To some extent, the knowledge that you will fish for a particular species of fish will govern your choice of tackle and soon you will discover that there are no great differences in the kind of tackle and approach required . . . though there are some.

Now while this book will guide you, there is no substitute for joining your local club or association. As a junior or as an adult beginner, you will find a friendly welcome and meet anglers who will be only too keen to help you learn more about coarse fishing. The major clubs and associations in Britain are affiliated to the National Federation of Anglers, for whom this book has been produced. By dropping a line (with a stamped addressed envelope) to the Federation's secretary at Haig House, 87 Green Lane, Derby, you can find out which is your nearest Federation-affiliated organisation.

Courses for anglers who want to teach beginners are now well established and this is leading to a nationwide network of coaches. Information about your nearest coach can be obtained from the National Anglers' Council, 5 Cowgate, Peterborough PE1 1LR. Meanwhile, make a resolution to read as much as you can about the sport. It has thriving weekly and monthly magazines and newspapers which offer basic information as well as details of the latest developments.

So much for general introductions. Let's get down to basics together now by considering first the fish you are going to catch and, especially, those which are likely to be most interesting.

THE CATCH

As we see it, the following should be considered the major species . . . barbel, bream, carp, chub, perch, pike, roach and tench. Let's take a look at them individually to discover their sporting potential and to see how their habits help us catch them.

The Barbel

The barbel grows big. The current British record is a fish of 13 lbs 12 ozs caught from the Hampshire Avon by Joseph Day in 1962, though there have been accurate reports of barbel in Britain in excess of 17 lbs. The barbel is also tough, its torpedo shape making it the gamest fighter in the entire family of coarse fish. A fish of the river, the barbel was once less well distributed than it is today when, thanks to far-sighted re-stocking operations, it is there to be caught in many more rivers than it once was. The rivers which offer the best chance of barbel sport are the Hampshire Avon, Dorset Stour, Thames, Severn and the rivers which make up the Yorkshire Ouse network. The barbel is a bottom-feeding fish which prefers gravelly runs close to weed-beds. Knowing this helps the angler decide where to look for them and how to present his bait to them. Barbel are easier to catch in summer, their appetites declining as the temperature drops below 50 degrees Fahrenheit. Beginners would be advised to use a reel line of not less than 6 lbs breaking strain if barbel of 6 lbs or more are known to live in the river being fished.

Scientific name: *Barbus barbus*

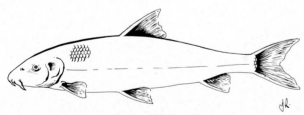

Fig. 1.   The Barbel

The Bream

The bream is the complete opposite of the barbel. Where the latter like the bustling power of streamy water, the bream, especially the biggest ones, are found in still waters and sluggish rivers, the most typical examples of the latter being those in the Fens of Eastern England. The record bream weighed 12 lbs 14 ozs and was caught in the Suffolk Stour in 1971. The only thing the bream might be said to have in common with the barbel is that it, too, is basically a bottom feeder, a fact which, again, tells the beginner where best to put his hookbait. Bream tend to live in large shoals, which means that, if you catch one, there are likely to be many more nearby. During the daylight hours, the most fish are generally found in the deepest parts of that water. If they are not actually in the deepest water when you first start to fish, they will soon move into it if they become aware of danger. Bream can signal their presence to anglers in a number of ways . . . first by the clouds of colour they cause in the water when feeding avidly, and sometimes by the large bubbles which rise to the surface at such times. During the mild weather they can often be seen splashing on the surface as they rise, flip their tails and shoot down again. It follows that it's always a good thing to look for these signs *before* tackling up at any bream water. As bream are distributed over much of Britain, they can offer the best chance of a big fish

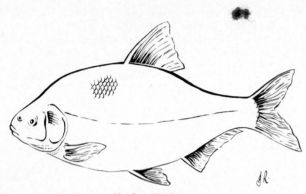

Fig. 2.   The Bream

for many anglers. There is the added attraction that bream will feed all year round, though they become less active at temperatures below 45 degrees. They are easiest to catch when the water is coloured, either after rain or strong wind. The day should preferably be cloudy, for bream feed less well in bright sunshine—unless the water is coloured.

Scientific name: *Abramis brama*

The Carp

At 44 lbs, the record carp caught by Richard Walker from Redmire Pool in 1952 is the biggest fish in the coarse fish record list. Carp have a natural preference for still water, and it is certainly lakes, ponds and pits which produce most of the big fish which are caught. The beginner, in our experience, will only encounter large carp if he fishes mixed fisheries where carp are one of the many species in the water. The River Nene around Peterborough is a good example. Really successful carp anglers are very dedicated men, who often fish scores of hours for just one bite from a big fish. Their methods are specialised, too, and, in our view, the beginner would be advised to steer clear of this kind of approach to carp until he has developed a basic knowledge of general coarse fishing. Like barbel and bream, the carp is also a bottom-feeder which is not keen to feed in low temperatures. Latterly, more and more waters—usually ponds or lakes—have been stocked with carp and the fish are now, as a result, much more

Fig. 3.   The Carp

widely distributed than in the past. Because of their size, carp demand the use of stronger lines, 10 lbs breaking strain being popular with anglers after carp weighing 20 lbs and more. Many baits—especially big ones like whole new potato—have been used to tempt carp, but recently many carp experts have begun working on the theory that smaller baits, like maggot, might be more worthy of consideration than in the past.

Scientific name: *Cyprinus carpio*

The Chub

Though the chub is occasionally found in still water, it is generally accepted as a fish of the faster-flowing rivers and is a formidable adversary for the angler. Because of disputes over past captures the British Record Fish Committee declared the record for chub open for claims and the record is now held by a Hampshire Avon fish of 7 lbs 6 ozs, though many in excess of this weight have been reported. Chub can be big. They're bustling, broad-shouldered fish, which fight powerfully once hooked. They are rated among the shyest of the coarse fish. A heavy footfall is all that is needed to frighten a chub. Being able to overcome the natural shyness of these fish is one of the greatest challenges for the coarse fisherman. It follows from this that chub like cover. An overhanging willow, for instance, or sunken tree roots, are likely hiding places, and these are the most obvious spots for the chub angler. In some cases the cover which attracts the chub

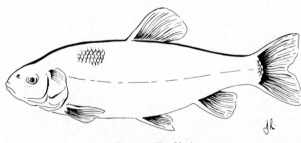

Fig. 4.   The Chub

can also become camouflage for the angler as he presents his bait. Anglers should conceal themselves as much as possible behind bankside growth. Chub will eat to a wider variety of bait than any other fish. Almost anything *might* catch a chub. Fishing for them is often a roving game, for chub live in small shoals, and once a couple of fish have been taken, it can be hard to persuade the rest that what you have got to offer is to their advantage. Chub will feed at much lower temperatures than many other coarse fish, though it seems equally true that the lower the temperature the smaller the bait which should be offered to them.
Scientific name: *Leuciscus cephalus*

The Perch

The perch is not a particularly popular fish with experienced coarse fishermen, its predatory behaviour being blamed for upsetting sport with other species. Be this as it may, the perch must be counted a very useful fish for the beginner, for he will surely find that these voracious feeders can often be caught when others cannot, especially if the hookbait being offered is worm. The currently accepted record perch is a fish of 4 lbs 12 ozs taken by S. F. Baker from Oulton Broad in 1962, though bigger perch have been reported over the years. In recent years, perch have become scarce due, it's believed, to a disease of some kind which spread through most parts of the country. However, stocks are now building up again and could be back to normal within ten years. Perch are widely distributed throughout Britain, being found in rivers, lakes, streams, ponds—almost everywhere, in fact, where there's water. Like chub, they're all-year-round feeders, though it's true to say that the warmer the weather the nearer to the surface perch are likely to be encountered. Because they are predators, perch lurk in places which offer the kind of 'hide' from which they can pounce on their prey. Sunken trees, weedbeds, bridge and jetty supports are typical of the kind of places tenanted by perch. It is said—and

Fig. 5.   The Perch

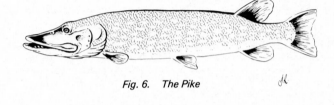

Fig. 6.   The Pike

it's a theory we share—that the biggest perch in any water are most often found in the deepest part of it.

Scientific name: *Perca fluviatilis*

The Pike

Regarded by many anglers as the king of the freshwater predators, the pike is, for many, the first big fish they catch in their angling careers, sometimes because it has grabbed a fish the angler has just hooked. Following a dispute, the pike record has been declared open and claims are now permitted for fish with a minimum weight of 35 lbs. As many fish have been reported in excess of this weight, it is likely there will be a fair number of claims. Like carp, pike call for specialised techniques if they are to be caught regularly. Like perch, pike are found in all kinds of waters. Even small ponds can contain pike in excess of 20 lbs, as regular headlines in the angling press demonstrate. There are three basic methods used to catch pike. The first is livebaiting, in which, as its name suggests, a live fish is offered on the hook. The second is deadbaiting. Dead coarse fish and even sea fish (mackerel, sprat and herring) are used and many anglers claim that these attract bigger fish. The third method involves artificial baits—spinners and plugs.

Scientific name: *Esox lucius*

The Roach

The roach is probably the most popular fish of all with coarse fishermen, even though the biggest specimen ever caught only weighed 4 lbs 1 oz. The record is held by Richard Jones who took his fish from a Nottingham gravel pit in June 1975. Why is the roach so popular? It is widespread, exists in large numbers in both flowing and still waters and can be caught by many varied methods and baits. And it fights very well, considering it is by no means a big fish. A roach of 1 lb is rated a good one. A roach of 2 lbs is reckoned outstanding. Many good roach anglers fish all their

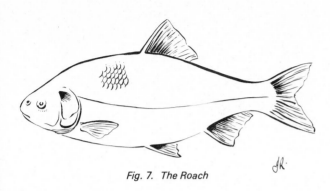

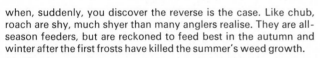

Fig. 7. The Roach

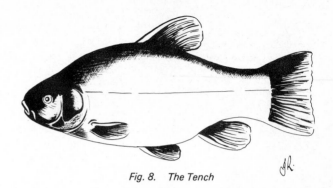

Fig. 8. The Tench

when, suddenly, you discover the reverse is the case. Like chub, roach are shy, much shyer than many anglers realise. They are all-season feeders, but are reckoned to feed best in the autumn and winter after the first frosts have killed the summer's weed growth.

Scientific name: *Rutilus rutilus*

The Tench

These are the tough guys of still and sluggish waters, putting up a fight pound for pound which compares well with even the barbel. For this reason, tench offer very attractive fishing. The biggest caught weighed 10 lbs 1 oz and was taken by Lewis Brown of Peterborough from a brick pit near his home in August 1975. The tench is a beautiful fish, its olive flanks which feel like silk to the touch and its pinkish eyes being one of the most coveted sights in coarse fishing. Though found in some of the sluggish rivers in Eastern England, tench are best sought in lakes, ponds and gravel pits, these kind of waters having produced all our biggest tench. Tench are warm-weather fish and are most active from the start of the coarse fishing season, in June, to the end of August. The best time to try and catch them is just before dusk and just after dawn. In many waters, tench have stopped feeding by 9 a.m. Tench are bottom feeders and, like bream, often reveal their presence by sending up bubbles from the bed of the lake or river. The best place to fish for tench is usually close to weed beds. Where no weeds are present, the tench are more likely to be caught close to the bank. The earlier in the season you fish for tench, the more likely it is they will be in shallow water. As the weeks of the season continue, they move into deeper water.

Scientific name: *Tinca tinca*

The other species

As we said earlier, there are other coarse fish which are not of such great interest to the angler as those we have just been discussing, fish which will all too often be encountered by accident rather than design. These are:

Bleak (scientific name: *Alburnus alburnus*): a small sprat-like fish most commonly found in streamy rivers.

Crucian carp (*Carassius carassius*): a miniature version of the carp, crucians have no barbules. Not widely distributed and mostly found in still waters.

Dace (*Leuciscus leuciscus*): a delightful river fish sometimes mistaken for a roach, at others for a small chub. The dace is most at home on gravelly shallows. Fished for with fine tackle, it can offer most satisfying sport.

Eel (*Anguilla anguilla*): found everywhere and not popular with the majority of anglers, not least because it frequently swallows the hook.

Grayling (*Thymalus thymalus*): not nearly as widely distributed as the other river fish, the grayling is most often found in the faster-flowing and cleaner rivers. It prefers a gravel bed close to weeds. Its greatest advantage to anglers is that it will feed at temperatures much lower than most other coarse fish.

Rudd (*Scardinius erythropthalmus*): A fish commonly confused with the roach, rudd have brilliant red fins. They prefer still waters and have the reputation of being surface feeders in warm weather. The easiest way to tell a rudd from a roach? The latter has a protruding top lip, while in the rudd it's the bottom lip which is dominant.

Ruffe (*Acerina cernua*): A tiddler species found in rivers and lakes. Can be a nuisance when a small bait—such as maggot—is being fished.

Zander (*Stizostedion lucioperca*): A fish which looks like a cross between a pike and a perch, but which is a species in its own right. The zander is only found at present in the Great Ouse system but is gradually spreading to other waters. The record fish weighed 15 lbs 5 ozs.

Rarities

The following rare fish are extremely unlikely to be encountered by beginners . . . burbot, catfish, char, lamprey, powan, schelly and vendace.

Spawning Habits of Coarse Fish

All coarse fish spawn sometime in the period from spring to early summer, the time varying from place to place. Usually fish in the warmer water spawn first. To protect fish from angling at these times, there is a closed season in England and Wales, though not in Scotland and Ireland. The close season begins at midnight on March 14 and ends at midnight on June 15, the only exception being Yorkshire where the close season begins at midnight on February 28, ending at midnight on May 31.

The link between the tackle you need and the water you are to fish

If a beginner inspects a practised angler's fishing tackle, his first reaction could be bewilderment at the many items in the collection. In fact, as we hope to demonstrate, the beginner's needs can be kept extremely basic. Several general principles are worth mention under this heading. Always in your early days, try and fish a water close to hand. When you have made your choice, ask yourself what kind of water it is. Is it still, i.e. a lake or a pond ? Or is it a river—and therefore a moving water ? Settle this question *before* setting out to buy your first fishing tackle for the type of water you fish will have considerable bearing on the sort of tackle you should get.

If there is an angler among your acquaintances then the right kind of advice should be immediately available. If not, the best person to consult is your local tackle dealer. They're a friendly breed and they'll be only too happy to offer you help about other aspects of your angling debut. There's sense in it, too. A tackle dealer who does a good job in putting a beginner on the right track could enjoy his custom for years—even a lifetime.

Clearly cost can be a stumbling block and there's no doubt that the cost of fishing tackle is rising as alarmingly as so many other things. If your pocket is shallow so be it. But if you can afford to buy some of the better items (which, of course, are always more expensive) it's a wise move. Remember, too, that most of the dearer items, like rods and reels, will last a long time if properly looked after. Quality counts in fishing tackle just as it does in other fields.

The pages which follow should help you further with the problems of deciding what is going to be the right tackle for you.

THE TACKLE IN DETAIL

The Rod

This, clearly, is one of the most important items in any angler's armoury. For coarse fishing, there are many different types and at first sight the choice must seem daunting to any beginner. He will probably be looking for a general-purpose rod, one which will be effective in all circumstances. Sadly such things do not exist. What you have to do is try and achieve an approximation to this ideal. For an adult, we recommend a 13 ft rod. Rods which are too short can impose insurmountable difficulties so think of 12 ft as the minimum. The rod should be a three piece (for easy carrying) and made of hollow as opposed to solid glass for the former has a much better action. It's easier to cast with and you get better fun playing a fish. When it comes to the juvenile angler, we urge simply the longest rod the child can comfortably handle. We'd say

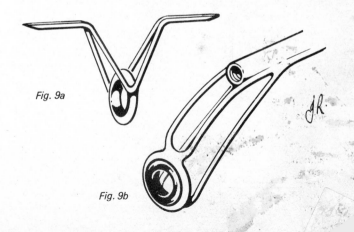

Fig. 9a

Fig. 9b

a minimum of 10 ft and add that purchasing parents should remember that their child is growing . . . not shrinking ! The rod you buy should have what are called stand-off rings (Fig 9a) for these make casting very much easier, especially in wet weather. It should also have what is known as a screw-in end ring (Fig 9b), this to accommodate bite indicators called swing tips and quiver tips, of which more later. Of the fish we have mentioned on earlier pages, the rod we have recommended will not be suitable for pike or carp. Stronger rods of special design are needed for this purpose and must be bought separately. Best, we think, to find out how well you use your 13-footer before considering further investments of this kind. And we must repeat . . . the more you spend the better the rod you will get.

The Reel

Once not so long ago the most universally used reel among coarse fishermen was the centre pin. This consisted of a revolving drum which contained the line, the drum rotating on a central spindle. It's a beautiful piece of equipment to use and there are still anglers around who make the use of one look like poetry in motion. But to the beginner, we say . . . don't buy one. You'll have quite enough problems to solve without trying to control a centre pin. The reel to go for is a fixed spool (Fig 10). Today, there are two types of fixed spools, known as open faced and closed faced. The latter is an extremely good piece of equipment. It is at its best when used to fish moving water but we think the beginner would be wise to set his sights on a good quality open face fixed spool. The beauty of this reel compared with, say, the centre pin is that it will permit a beginner to cast a considerable distance with relative ease, a singular advantage as you will discover. It is the best general purpose reel on the market. As with the rod, try to get the best you can afford.

Fig. 10.

The Line

Almost all coarse anglers today use nylon monofilament line. This is sold in a number of breaking strains, the line becoming thicker the stronger it is. The two commonest errors made by beginners are that they buy line which is far too strong for the fish they hope to catch and, secondly, they don't buy enough. To discuss the first point first. Beginners seem to think that if they are likely to catch fish weighing 4 lbs they must use line which has a breaking strain of at least 4 lbs, with 6 lbs fish, 6 lbs breaking strain and so on. In fact, thick (i.e. strong) line is more difficult to cast, more difficult to control, is more easily seen by the fish and limits the number of bites likely. An ideal line for a beginner, in our view, would be one of 3 lbs breaking strain. Eventually, as experience comes, most beginners will use $2\frac{1}{2}$ lbs line. If, however, he is fishing water which contains big fish, like barbel and chub, this will not be strong enough and we recommend 4 lbs. Such lines, of course, should not be used for carp or pike.

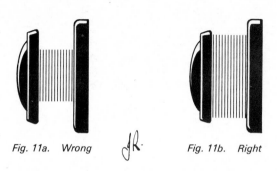

Fig. 11a. Wrong   Fig. 11b. Right

Beginners seem to think that as they are going to cast, for instance, 15 yards, then 25 yards of line will be enough. In fact, it will be far from enough and will impede casting ability to a level of maddening frustration. The spool of some fixed-spool reels can contain as much as 250 yards of line. The amount varies according to the breaking strain of the line placed on the spool. Under no circumstances should you attempt to fish with less than 100 yards of line and even then the line must be correctly loaded on to the spool of the reel. This is one of the commonest failings by angling beginners. The line should, in fact, fill the spool almost to the lip (see Figs 11a and 11b). This will allow the line to pull easily off the spool when the cast is made. If the spool is inadequately filled (see Fig 11a) the line will catch on the lip of the spool, considerably reducing the distance which can be comfortably cast. An under-filled spool also restricts the accuracy of the cast.

Floats

These are perhaps the most confusing item of all. Most tackle shops carry a stock of several hundred—even thousands. Which to buy can be a very confusing question. The purpose of the float is to present the bait to the fish at the right depth in the water and to signal a bite. Some floats are designed for river fishing, the remainder for still water. These two patterns (see Figs 12a and 12b) spell out the basic principles. In still water, the buoyancy of the float is concentrated at the bottom of the stem, by using a cork or balsa body (Fig 12a). In a float for river fishing, the buoyancy is concentrated near the top as in the Avon float (Fig 12b). With the still water pattern, the aim is to provide stability against wind and surface drag, in running water the float must ride the current without being dragged beneath the surface. As a general principle, all still water floats are fastened to the line by the bottom ring, what anglers call 'bottom only' floats.

Running water floats are ideally fished top and bottom, the line being locked to the tip of the float with a small piece of valve rubber. This can, however, only be done effectively when the wind is blowing in an upstream direction. Whenever it's downstream, the river float must also be fished 'bottom only'. An exception is the sliding float, used to fish deep water. This float, as its name suggests, slides up the line after the cast until it is held at the required depth by a stop knot. This, however, is a difficult technique for a beginner and we advise you to ignore it in your early days. When faced with such water, we'd recommend a leger . . . of which more later. From these general principles, it is possible to impose some kind of order on the array of floats you find in your tackle shop. The resemblance of the floats you see to the basic patterns described will tell you whether the float is meant for still or running water.

From floats to float sizes. Let's say you have wisely decided to buy an Avon float for river work. When you look further you

Fig. 12a.
Still water

Fig. 12b.
River pattern

suddenly discover there are big ones and small ones. So which do you need? Each float is adjusted to 'cock' in the water by the addition of weight placed on the line in the form of split shot. This weight is necessary to achieve casting distance and to speed the descent of the bait in the water. As winds, and the effect they have on the distance you can cast, vary and as currents vary in such a way that they can affect the speed a bait will fall in the water, it follows that a variety of different sized floats of the same type is needed to allow you to cope with varying conditions. To give an example, you may be fishing an Avon float carrying four BB shot with complete control when the wind becomes stronger. Suddenly you find you can no longer cast to the spot where the fish are feeding, or that your float is dragging sideways. All you have to do is change to a bigger Avon float (say one carrying 6 BB) until the necessary distance is again achievable and you are again in control of the tackle. It should follow from this that you must buy a 'family' of the basic floats if you, too, are to have this advantage. One float of any pattern is never enough.

The basic materials used in float manufacture are cane, reed and quill (especially peacock quill) for float stems, and balsa, cork and, latterly, polystyrene for float bodies. Some of these materials are more buoyant than others—they need more weight to cock them. Peacock quill, for instance, is more buoyant than cane, so you will readily see that peacock rides a current better than cane.

The wise angler thinks about the colour of his float tip before buying. When the sun is on the water, what is called a 'white' water, a black tip is more easily seen and eye-strain avoided. Where the surface is dark because it's shaded by trees, for example, a white tip is to be preferred. These are the basic colours, but others—like fluorescent red or orange—are also used, especially when fishing at long range. Aim to find out as soon as you can what colours suit *your* eyes for different coloured water and stick to these, for not everybody is the same in this most important respect.

What types of float should you buy? It is impossible to be completely accurate because rivers and still water vary so much around the country, but a good basic selection would be as follows...

For STILL water (i.e. ponds, lakes, gravel pits, etc.)

The Reverse Crowquill (Fig 13a)

This, as its name suggests, is a quill fished upside down, the float ring being fitted to the thicker end of the quill. Fished in this style, it means that the slim end of the quill is at the surface. The slimmer tip is more easily submerged by a bite than the thick end would be if it was up top. This is a light float for use at short range.

The Dart (Fig 13b)

This is a cane-stemmed float with a slim balsa body loaded at its base with brass rod. The latter means the float can be cast a fair distance while carrying a comparatively small shot load below. In this way light tackle can be offered to fish at some range. The Dart is also an extremely useful float when fishing canals.

The Straight Peacock (Fig 13c)

Another self-descriptive name. This float is simply a piece of peacock quill with a ring attached at the bottom end. It is best held on the line by pinching on a shot either side of the float ring (known as the 'locked shot' method). These shots aid casting in the same way as the loading in the Dart. They also enable you to fish with light shots on the terminal length.

The Waggler (Fig 13d)

One of the most famous of floats, this is simply a straight peacock with a balsa or cork body added at the lower end. This body enables the float to carry more shot than the straight peacock and

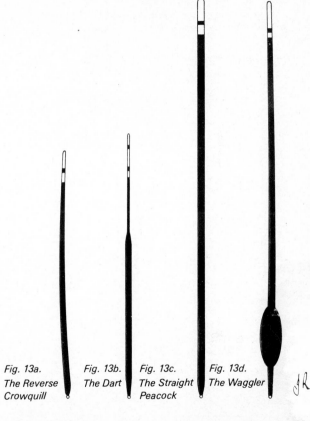

Fig. 13a.
The Reverse Crowquill

Fig. 13b.
The Dart

Fig. 13c.
The Straight Peacock

Fig. 13d.
The Waggler

it can therefore be cast further. In other words, it's the long range still water float. The Waggler is also useful on rivers when the wind is blowing downstream, but is never cast so far in running water as in still water.

Floats for STREAMY water (i.e. rivers and flowing canals).

The Stick (Fig 14a)

This is another famous float. It consists of a cane stem with a balsa tip spliced into it thus giving the float buoyancy at the tip. The Stick is an extremely sensitive float which is best used when the wind is upstream. A wind of any real strength makes the Stick difficult to control and this tells you that it is something of a fair-weather float.

The Avon (Fig 14b)

This is the float you use when conditions are too tough for a Stick. The Avon consists of a cane stem with a balsa body near the tip, another way of giving a float 'tip' buoyancy. The Avon is a classic of its kind, the pattern having been in use for decades, with little likelihood of it being superseded.

The Ducker (Fig 14c)

This float might best be described as a reverse Avon . . . because it is made in precisely the same way, except that the body is now at the base of the stem. The Ducker is used when the wind is *downstream*, a wind every angler comes to hate, and is fixed bottom only to enable you to sink your line under the surface out of the way. Whereas the Avon has a cane stem, the Ducker stem is usually of quill—to provide additional buoyancy in the tip.

The Waggler (Fig 13d)

Already mentioned as a still water float, the Waggler is also useful in a river in a downstream wind as an alternative to the Ducker. Many anglers these days prefer the Waggler to the Ducker, finding it easier to control. While floats may be 'checked' in an upstream wind to induce bites by making the bait lift in the water,

neither the Waggler nor the Ducker may be checked in this way for this would lead to the immediate submersion of the float and the register of a 'false' bite. The moral: Duckers and Wagglers in rivers in a downstream wind must be fished at the speed of the water.

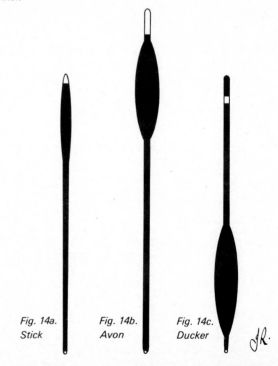

Fig. 14a.
Stick

Fig. 14b.
Avon

Fig. 14c.
Ducker

Float Postscript

Almost every float falls into one or other of the categories just mentioned from the design viewpoint. By comparing those you are offered with the patterns shown here, you can realise immediately what kind of condition that float is meant to cope with.

How to Weight Your Float

This is done by means of split shot—soft, circular pieces of lead with a split in them (Fig 15). The line is placed in position in the slit and the shot held in place by pinching it between the fingers. Any shot you buy should be soft enough to squeeze shut with the fingers and soft enough to be opened with your thumb nail. Be warned: a lot of shot is not this soft and should be rejected for it will make tackle changes difficult and time-wasting.

Fig. 15.

Shot are bought in a number of sizes (see Fig 15 again) as follows:

Swan, AAA, BB, No 1, No 2, No 4, No 6, No 8 (this latter often being referred to as 'dust' shot because of its smallness).

In calculating the amount of shot needed to cock a float, a useful yardstick is that one Swan=two AAA approx, one AAA= two BB approx and so on.

Many floats are sold nowadays with the shotting capacity printed on them. Be warned again: these are usually approximate. Note, too, that if a float calls for two Swan, this does not usually mean you use two actual swan shot, simply that the weight of the total amount of shot to be used to make up your shotting pattern is *equivalent* to two swan.

Hooks

Clearly, these are one of the most important tackle items of all. Like shot, hooks are sold in different sizes, the bigger ones being used for bigger baits (like bread flake), the smaller ones for smaller morsels (like maggot). Beginners all too often think that it is the size of fish which might be caught which governs the size to be used. This is only sometimes the case. It is usually the size of the bait which decides the size of the hook to be used.

Hooks are generally sold in the following sizes, (Fig 16): 1, 2, 3, 4, 6, 8, 10, 12, 14, 16, 18, 20.

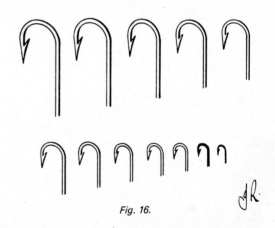

Fig. 16.

The smaller the number the bigger the hook. Beginners would be advised to get a stock of 16s, 14s, and 12s, the smaller hooks for maggot and caster, the bigger ones for bait such as bread flake and worms.

Not only are there different *sizes* of hooks, there are different *types*. The beginner is urged not to get too involved in these differences but simply to buy forged hooks. They are not the most elegant, but they are the strongest—and that's important at this stage in your fishing.

Hooks also vary in the way they are fixed to the line. There are eyed hooks, spade-end hooks and what are called hooks-to-nylon, the latter being the most expensive. As the names of the first two suggest, an eyed hook (Fig 17a) is tied to the line by means of the eye, the spade (Fig 17b) by means of the blade at the top of the hook shank. The hook-to-nylon (Fig 17c) is sold ready tied to a length of nylon. It offers a neater tie. With any hook, a reduction in the strength of the hook length—3 lbs reel line linked, for instance, to a 2 lbs hook length—can give advantages. Smaller hooks 'hang' better on a lighter line. The latter gives better presentation, especially when fish are shy. Bottom-feeding fish can suck the bait into their mouths more easily with a lighter terminal length.

And this (Fig 18) is how you tie a spade-end hook to your line.

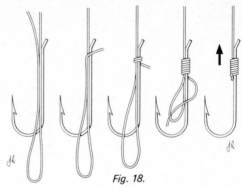

Fig. 18.

Should you decide you prefer eyed hooks, the knot to use is the tucked half blood knot (Fig 19) which is tied like this . . .

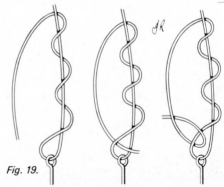

Fig. 19.

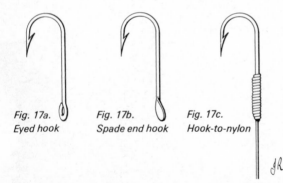

Fig. 17a.
Eyed hook

Fig. 17b.
Spade end hook

Fig. 17c.
Hook-to-nylon

The nylon on the hook-to-nylon is connected to the reel line by means of the water knot (Fig 20). This is *the* basic knot for linking two pieces of line together. It has the added merit of being the strongest. As you will discover the water knot has other uses, one of which will become apparent when we discuss the technique known as legering.

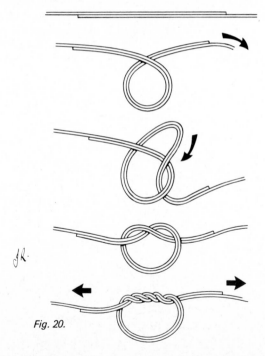

Fig. 20.

Now so far, it is apparent that coarse fishermen catch fish by using a float. But there's another regularly used technique called *legering*. The beginner should think of legering whenever he finds difficulty in presenting his bait with a float. A good yardstick would be this . . . the closer you are fishing to the bank the more likely it is you will succeed with a float. And here's another . . . the shallower the water the more likely it is that the float will be best.

Whether to float fish or leger can be defined further as follows. Legering will become necessary (a) when the water is too deep to be fished with a float other than a slider (which we recommend beginners should not use), (b) when the place to be fished is beyond casting range of a float, and (c) when you want to present a stationary bait in a flowing water.

The most commonly used (and most efficient) end tackle for legering is known as the fixed paternoster. It consists of a lead weight known as an Arlesey bomb (Fig 21) fished on a nylon boom with the hook length below it.

Fig. 21.

The paternoster rig when set up looks like this ... (Fig 22a).

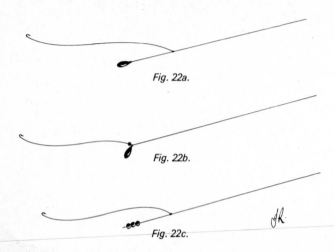

Fig. 22a.

Fig. 22b.

Fig. 22c.

The shot leger (Fig 22c). This is the same as the paternoster already shown except that split shots are used instead of an Arlesey bomb to reduce the resistance of the tackle. Before the split shots are pinched on to the boom, a knot should be tied in the end of it to stop them slipping off. It's worth noting that if you are paternostering with a bomb and find it's not quite heavy enough, the addition of a split shot to the boom (rather than a change of bomb) may be all that's needed to adjust the balance.

Arlesey bombs are sold in varying sizes, the commonest being $\frac{1}{8}$ oz, $\frac{1}{4}$ oz, $\frac{1}{2}$ oz, $\frac{3}{4}$ oz and 1 oz. The one you are likely to use most is the $\frac{1}{2}$ oz. The size of bomb selected should always be the smallest that will allow you to cast where you want or, in running water, the smallest that will hold bottom without rolling too much. Remember, too, that bigger bombs cause more disturbance and can frighten fish away.

The Arlesey bomb is fixed to the boom with the tucked half blood knot, the hook according to the type being used (i.e. eyed, spade-end or hook-to-nylon). The tying of the boom to the reel line is done by means of the water knot. Other end rigs which can be used for legering are ...

The running leger (Fig 22b). In this case the bomb is simply threaded directly on to the reel line. It is prevented from running down to foul the hook by a small split shot pinched on two feet above the hook. A good dodge is to put a piece of valve rubber on the line above the shot to act as a shock absorber. This prevents the stop shot slipping.

There are three methods of bite indication when legering which should concern the beginner. The first of these is . . .

Rod-top legering. With this method the line is threaded through the rod rings and the fixed paternoster or running leger rig made up on the end. When the bait has been cast into the water and the line tightened to the bomb by turning the reel, the angler watches the rod top. This develops a sudden and distinct bend at the extreme tip when a fish takes the bait and pulls the line.

Swing-tipping. With this method, a bite indicator, called a swing tip, is fitted into the screw in the top ring we urged you to have fitted on your rod. The line is threaded through the rod rings *and* the rings on the swing tip. Once again the paternoster is added at the end. After the bomb has been cast in, the line is tightened to it so that the swing tip hangs just off vertical. When a fish takes the tip will pull forward (if the fish is swimming away from you) or fall back (if the fish is coming towards you). The swing tip is at its most effective in still or sluggish waters.

Quiver-tipping. This is another bite indicator fitted to the screw in end ring of your rod. It is like a slender extension to the rod. In other words, this is a more sophisticated form of rod-top legering. It simply means that with a quiver tip the end of your rod is thinner and it therefore bends more easily under light pressure from a fish grabbing your bait. While the quiver tip is useful on still waters when it's extremely windy, it is mostly used on rivers. Experienced anglers usually own two or more quiver tips of varying thicknesses and invariably use the thinnest conditions allow.

At your tackle shop, then, you should buy a swing tip and a quiver tip. It should be added that, while these aids will work on the end of your 13 ft rod, you will be able to use these methods much more efficiently if your pocket permits the purchase of a special swing tip rod. The best length is 9 ft 6 ins, and if the rod has a screw-in end ring, it can be effectively used for both swing and quiver tipping.

Other items are needed which are best summed up under the heading of

Accessories

These, in alphabetical order, are . . .

Banksticks: Metal sticks with a screw top for supporting rod rests and keepnets. The alloy type are lightest.

Catapult: Used for getting softly mixed bait or maggots further than they can be thrown by hand.

Disgorger: A tool which enables you to play dentist when fish swallow the hook. Your tackle dealer will show you the different types and how they work. The Sheffield type is recommended.

Keepnet: A long net (usually cylindrical) in which your catch is kept before being released alive to fight another day. The best types (because they damage the fish less) are the knotless keepnets. *NB:* These are already obligatory in some areas.

Landing Net: An obvious need. Some like them triangular, others, circular. We don't think it matters so long as it's big enough *and* collapsible. Also needed—a handle for the net, preferably telescopic.

Mixing Bowl: A small plastic bowl (of the type used for washing up) for mixing groundbait in.

Plummet: A small but vital piece of equipment needed to measure the depth of the water.

Polaroid spectacles: Extremely useful for spotting fish in advance of fishing, especially in clear water. Also helpful in preventing eyestrain during prolonged spells of float fishing in bright sunlight.

Rod Rest Sold complete or as an attachment to a bankstick Make sure you buy one which allows free movement of the line. (see Fig 23).

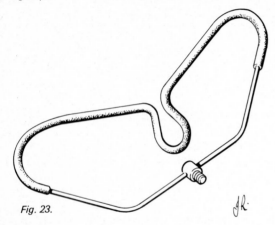

Fig. 23.

Scissors: A small but obviously important item.

Umbrella: An expensive piece of equipment but in our climate, a good investment. The bigger the better.

The list could be longer but we've stuck to basics. We should add that you'll want a hold-all to carry things like rods, banksticks, brolly and landing net handle and something else to carry the rest. A basket is the general choice but many now favour the custom-built seat carriers which have come on the market.

Your tackle shopping complete, what else do you need? Without any doubt the next most important thing is . . .

BAIT

In these days of constantly developing techniques for coarse fishing, there is developing, too, an almost bewildering variety of hookbaits to go with them. Faced with a comprehensive list, any beginner is bound to feel confused. In fact, a wide range of baits is not necessary to get well and truly started on the road to coarse fishing success. A knowledge of just four is, in our view, enough to see any budding coarse fisherman through his apprenticeship.

These baits are . . .

Maggot, Caster, Worm and Bread

Let's take a look at them in that order and first . . .

Maggot. This is probably the most widely used bait of all, though these days it is being rapidly caught up by the caster. Maggots are the larvae of various types of fly. Those sold over tackle shop counters—the kind of most importance to the beginner—are the product of eggs laid by the bluebottle. The beauty of the maggot is that all species of coarse fish eat it readily . . . from big barbel down to small roach. This explains its great popularity.

Maggots—because of their size—are best fished on small hooks. They are offered singly (usually on an 18) or in multiples, double maggot being presented on a 16, three on a 14.

Care should be taken putting maggots on the hook, the aim being not to 'burst' the maggot, allowing body fluid to be released. The best way to do this safely (Fig 24) is to take the maggot between thumb and forefinger near the head and squeeze it gently. This will cause a piece of muscular tissue near the head to stand out from the body. Nick the maggot on to the hook through this piece of tissue.

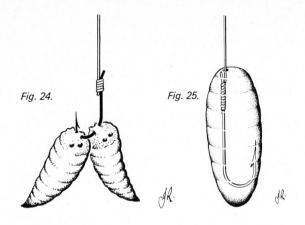

Fig. 24.

Fig. 25.

chrysalis). Such casters are hooked so that the hook is 'buried' inside them (Fig 25). The hook point is pushed through the upper (i.e., the head end) of the caster and turned so that the shank is sticking vertically upwards. This is gently tapped with the tip of the forefinger until it is encased in the caster, the finished result looking like the diagram. This 'burying' of the caster is a bit of a tricky operation for a beginner but one well worth persevering with for with the hook concealed in this way fish are more likely to take the bait freely. When the fish are feeding greedily, however, the caster can be hooked on so that the point of the hook is just protruding through the shell of the caster.

Like maggots, casters can be fished in multiples, this most often being the case when anglers are trying to catch bigger fish than can be taken with the single caster. Multiple casters are used for sizable fish like chub or barbel. In this case, the caster is hooked on like a maggot, two casters being offered on a 16, three on a 14 and so on.

Casters. These are maggots in chrysalis form . . . but at a particular stage in their lives. Within a few hours of the chrysalis developing, it will float when thrown into the water and be useless as bait, because this will draw the fish to the surface where they are hard, if not impossible, to catch. In the early hours of their existence, however, chrysalis will *sink*. These are your casters, their merit being that you can throw them into the water and they will sink to the bottom. Chrysalis are kept in this 'sinking' condition by being separated as soon as they have developed and preserved in refrigerators. Casters can be an absolutely first class bait but beginners are warned that it is sometimes necessary to loose feed with them for an hour or even longer before the first bites develop. During this coaxing period, it is not wise to introduce any other form of feed . . . to do so is to confuse the fish.

Casters are best accommodated on long shanked hooks. A single caster is normally fished on an 18 (a 16 if it's a really big

Bread. The beginner is best advised to fish this bait in his early days in the form known as flake. Other ways of fishing bread exist but these are best left until one's basic angling training is completed. To fish flake, a new sliced loaf is required. From the centre of the slice, a piece of bread is removed, folded over the hook and squeezed tightly near the top of the shank to make it adhere. The diagrams (Fig 26) demonstrate how this is done.

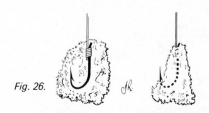

Fig. 26.

Flake is a big-fish bait. It can be fished on hooks ranging from a 16 on down to the biggest depending on the willingness of the fish to accept it. Many anglers, if they know big fish are present in the water, will spend the first hour offering nothing but flake in the hope of an early bonus big 'un. Generally, however, the calibre of fish present is examined first with baits like caster or maggot.

Worm. There are more than 20 different kinds of worm to be found in the British Isles. The angling beginner, however, would do best to concentrate on one kind only, the small red. Some of the others—especially lobworm—are trouble to come by and there'll be time enough later to try them. The small red, on the other hand, is easily obtained, being found in numbers in manure and compost heaps. Small reds fished singly can be confidently fished on 18, 16 or 14 hooks, the size of hook being dictated by the average size of worm. The worms can also be fished in multiples, twos, threes, and even fours, usually on 10 or 12 hooks.

The way a worm is hooked can often make a difference to the way the fish will respond. The commonest way is to hook the worm through the middle (Fig 27a). This allows it to produce its maximum wriggle in the water. Next it can be hooked in the head (Fig 27b). In this position, the worm is not so free to move but its efforts to do just that can sometimes bring it to the attention of the fish more quickly. Alternatively, the worm can be hooked in the tail (this position being simply Fig 27b in reverse). Thirdly, the worm can be double hooked (Fig 27c). In this form, the worm will appear to be a more solid morsel to the fish. In offering worm, the beginner should permutate the positions shown until he finds the one which will produce the most bites.

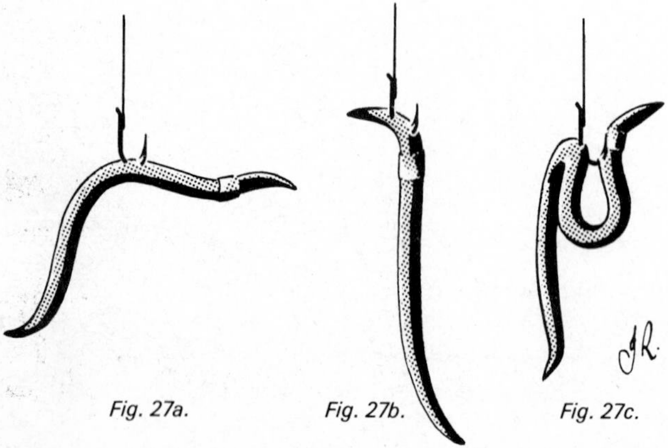

Fig. 27a.   *Fig. 27b.*   *Fig. 27c.*

Cocktails

These, as their name suggests, are combination baits. From the basic selection given above, the following cocktails are the best known and are well worth trying if these baits, fished singly, do not produce the desired result.

Maggot and Caster. This is a single maggot and caster hooked on together. Sometimes a maggot tipped with caster (i.e. the caster hooked on last) is better than the caster tipped with maggot.

Worm and Caster. A middle hooked red worm is tipped with a caster.

Worm and Maggot. A worm hooked in the same way, tipped with a maggot.

The good angler never neglects the 'cocktail' possibility. The cocktail will often take fish when a single bait fails.

Preserving Hookbaits

Knowing how to look after your hookbaits is just as important as knowing how to hook them . . . for all the baits mentioned are perishable.

Let's look at this question bait-by-bait and first . . .

Maggots. These are generally kept in plastic containers which can be bought at all tackle shops. The first priority is to always keep your containers clean. Indeed, this goes for all baits . . . fish prefer clean food much the same as we do. Always make certain that the airholes in the lid of the container are clear. Some do not offer enough ventilation so don't be afraid to punch more small holes in the lid yourself if you think this necessary. Maggots lacking sufficient ventilation will sweat and soon suffocate. Always keep maggots in a cool place, especially in hot weather. The concrete floor of a garage is ideal. Provided the tin is a round one, the maggots can be left with the lid off. Never leave maggots in direct sunlight. Not only does this make them turn to chrysalis faster, the maggots overheat and the resulting chrysalis are generally long and thin instead of short and fat. It follows that if all your maggots are not used, those left will turn to chrysalis. These should be separated as they develop with a small riddle for these can be your casters. They can be preserved in a refrigerator (set at not less than 34 deg F) or in clean cold water, the former being much the best method. Maggots, in normal temperatures, start to turn into chrysalis five to six days after being taken from the feed medium. The warmer it is the sooner they turn.

Casters. Much the same goes for casters as for maggots . . . which means keep them cool. Generally sold in plastic bags, these should be kept in the fridge or a cool cellar. If the bags begin to crinkle, this means the casters are absorbing the air in the bags too quickly. To rectify, open the bag and leave it open for half an hour then re-secure. The best casters are sold dry. Those sold in water have a tendency to go sour, a state in which they are useless for fishing.

Worms. Again the need is to keep the bait cool, preferably in a dark place. Small reds are best preserved in a bucket or largish plastic container in pig manure. If the latter is not obtainable, compost or spagnum moss (a fibrous moss found in the damp part of woods or bought from florists) may be used. Pig manure is best because the worms eat it.

Bread. New sliced bread produces the best flake. The tip here is to delay buying your bread until the last moment, best of all on the way to the water. Stale sliced bread is useless. It crumbles too easily and will not stay on the hook.

Maggots are sold by the pint. One pint should be enough for three hours fishing. Casters are also sold by the pint. Again, a pint should cover you for three hours. As worms are only used (at least at this stage in your fishing) as a hookbait, 50 should be ample for any trip. The bread? One sliced new loaf should be enough for any outing.

Good quality maggots like these can be safely preserved in plastic containers. *(Courtesy: ANS Ltd., Sheffield.)*

GROUNDBAIT

This is a vital commodity for any coarse fisherman and should always be carried. Though groundbait can take many forms (the word having a multiple meaning), most English coarse anglers simply mean ground stale bread when they refer to groundbait. It's bought from tackle shops and sold in three consistencies, fine, medium and coarse. The beginner would be advised to restrict his purchasing to the medium type as this will suffice for all his early needs. Groundbait can be used to fulfil three different functions.

These are:

(1) As a means of getting samples of the hookbait beyond the range these can be thrown by hand, the commonest use, in fact, of groundbait.

(2) As a means of creating an attractive cloud of colour in the water which, though edible, has no concentrated food value.

(3) As solid food designed to persuade madly feeding fish to keep on feeding where they are, this last being the least used function of the three.

A good question is how much groundbait should be used. Sadly, it is impossible to give any accurate answer for this can only be settled by the behaviour of the fish on the day. The best yardstick is that it's usually safe to give the fish a reasonable helping (say three tennis ball-sized lumps) at the start of a fishing stint and to add to this at intervals of 10 to 15 minutes on the 'little and often principle', little in this instance meaning golf ball size portions. All groundbait should contain samples of whatever hookbait is being fished, i.e. maggot, caster or worm. Bread is an exception for obvious reasons . . . groundbait *is* bread. Where fish are feeding madly—and this would be most typical where a big shoal of bream is chewing well—the groundbait will be absorbed very quickly. This is the kind of occasion when the groundbait is needed as food to keep the fish preoccupied in the place where you have found them.

It should have followed from the above that not only does groundbait get samples of the hookbait where you want them, it *concentrates* them in that place. From this, it should be realised that accuracy in throwing groundbait is one of the most important attributes any coarse fishermen must develop. The groundbait (and its additives) gets the fish interested, the hookbait, accurately cast to the same spot as the groundbait, hopefully proves that they are interested enough to be caught.

How do you mix groundbait? Take the plastic mixing bowl specified in our tackle list and put about an inch of water in it. Carefully tip in some groundbait and stir with the hands. The first mix should be sloppy. This can be stiffened by adding more groundbait (alternatively if it's too stiff it can be softened with more water). The consistency of the groundbait is right for use when the groundbait clings together when squeezed yet will break up when rolled on the palm of the hand.

The textures of groundbait. These are varied according to the type of water being fished and, sometimes, according to the behaviour of the fish. In still and sluggish water, the groundbait should be introduced as cloud. This means each ball is squeezed just hard enough to ensure that it will break up into particles on hitting the surface. If cloud bait has to be thrown any distance, a catapult will be needed, otherwise the balls of bait will break up in the air before reaching the desired destination. Where the waters we are discussing are deep and the bait must be thrown a long way, it will need to be squeezed harder to make sure it is reasonably near the bottom before breaking up. In streamy waters, like rivers, the groundbait is used as cloud where fish are feeding off the bottom and squeezed hard when it's necessary to get the bait deep down to bottom feeding fish before it breaks. From this it follows that once you have got the mix right, the texture can be varied at will simply by means of the degree of squeeze applied to the bait. It's worth adding that if additives (like maggots) are being put in the bait, the texture should be double checked after their addition.

How much groundbait is needed for an outing? This can vary but not less than 4 lbs should be a must, bearing in mind that any unused bait can be kept for another day.

Also to be counted under the heading of groundbait is loose feed. This, as its name suggests, is the introduction of helpings of the hookbait (maggot for instance) by throwing it into the water by hand, though still aiming to concentrate it in one area. The beginner will ask . . .when should I loose feed and when should I use groundbait? If the range at which you are fishing permits, loose feeding is often best unless the water is deep or fast flowing. Loose feed thrown into deep or fast water will not get where you want it — to the bottom. In these circumstances, its fall is helped by introducing it in groundbait. Don't forget, too, the possible use of your catapult when considering this question. It would be true to add that the species being sought can also play a part in your decision. Loose feeding is invariably best when roach fishing, for instance, if the circumstances are right. But for bottom feeding fish like bream or tench, groundbait is much more often necessary.

Sometimes both methods can pay. In feeding a far swim for fish like bream with groundbait, it's often wise to loose feed closer in then, if the distant swim fails to produce, you know that a second potential catching area is available to you.

So much, then, for the preliminaries of tackle and bait. Let us turn now to the practical aspects of coarse fishing by which we mean . . .

THE METHODS

Before any method—i.e. float fishing or legering—can be used you must know how to cast the bait into the water. This can be practised when you first get to the waterside but preferably in advance of your first expedition in a park or field.

Fit the fixed spool reel to the butt of the rod, making sure that it is so placed that the spool of the reel is facing in line with the rings and that it is sufficiently far up the butt for the latter to be held comfortably under the forearm. With rod and reel held like this, the base of the butt should extend about six inches below the elbow when the rod is held at the point where the reel has been positioned.

With the reel pick-up open, thread the line through the rod rings. The end tackle—either for float fishing or legering—is then added. For practice casting in a park, an Arlesey bomb tied on the line or a float fixed with two rubbers and some shot are sufficient.

At the start of the cast, the rod is held forward with two hands, one on the reel holding the line against the spool with the pick-up arm open, the other lower down the butt. Looked at from the angler's left (see Figs 28a, 28b and 28c) the rod at this moment will be in the eleven o'clock position (28a). The rod is then taken back. As it travels back the end tackle is beginning to lift (28b). At its furthest point back—about two o'clock—it is then impelled forward (28c) and by the time it has reached the eleven o'clock position again, the end tackle should be in a horizontal line from the tip parallel with the ground.

As soon as you feel the end tackle flexing the tip of the rod, continue the forward movement *at the same time releasing the finger from the reel spool*. This allows the tackle to take line from

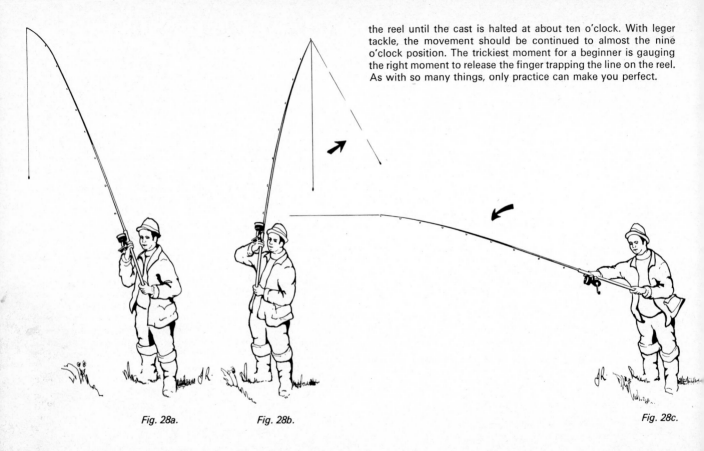

the reel until the cast is halted at about ten o'clock. With leger tackle, the movement should be continued to almost the nine o'clock position. The trickiest moment for a beginner is gauging the right moment to release the finger trapping the line on the reel. As with so many things, only practice can make you perfect.

Fig. 28a.

Fig. 28b.

Fig. 28c.

You now know how to cast so let's presume that your first efforts are going to be with a float.

FLOAT FISHING

Wherever a float is being used—whether in a lake or a river—the first task you must do is plumb the depth. This is done to find the exact depth of your fishing spot, and in most rivers this is likely to vary considerably across the expanse of water in front of you. Once you can establish the contour of the bottom you will then know where to cast to reach the deepest or, of course, shallowest, water. Fix the float on the line (the method being governed by the type of float being used, of which more later) and *attach the hook*. Let's say you guess the depth at 6 feet. Set the float at this depth and attach the plummet (see tackle requirements) to the hook. Cast to the chosen point. If the float does not rise to the surface, the water is deeper than you thought and the float must be adjusted accordingly. If the float tip shows in a way which suggests the tackle is nicely under tension, your guess was right. If, however, the float appears only to lie flat on the water, the tackle is set too shallow. Once the depth has been assessed the split shots are added to the line. If you wish the bottom shot to be positioned on the bed of the river or lake (what is called the 'laid on' position), you must remember to move the float further up the line to allow for this. It should be added that experienced anglers generally place the shots on the line *before* plumbing the depth. They do this because they have a pretty good idea of what's what before they start. The beginner would be advised to do it the way we have suggested.

Let's make another presumption now . . . that you are fishing still water, a lake, pond or gravel pit.

Still Water Float Fishing Patterns

It's a good general rule that the size of float you select will depend on the distance from the bank you wish to fish. The further out you want to cast the bigger the float will need to be if it is to 'cock' correctly in accordance with the weight being added to achieve the necessary distance. But split shots are added to float rigs for other reasons than to aid casting. The main one is to ensure that the bait is presented in a way the fish find acceptable. While many shotting patterns exist, the beginner is wise to stick to those that may be considered basic, moving on to variations when he has had some experience.

Three basic rigs are involved with achieving distance and beating the effect of the wind. In describing them, we have used three floats—the reverse quill, the straight peacock and the waggler—as examples. These, it is emphasised, are chosen to present the basic idea and not to suggest that other floats of a similar type may not be used if preferred.

Fishing at close range

A reverse quill (Fig 29a) is fixed bottom only (what's called a 'loose' float). A small shot, preferably a dust, is pinched on 18 ins above the hook and 24 ins above that all the rest of the shot needed to 'dot' the float. By 'dot', we mean that the minimum amount of float tip should be showing commensurate with your ability to see it. One of the commonest mistakes made by float fishing beginners is to have too much tip—say an inch or more—above the surface. It is not only unnecessary, it offers greater resistance for the fish to submerge. Getting the float 'dotted' also means that the tackle is perfectly balanced, i.e. the addition of just one more small shot would submerge it. This is your guarantee of sensitivity. The pattern just described—a classic from which many others stem—should enable you to fish fairly lightly up to two rod lengths out from the bank.

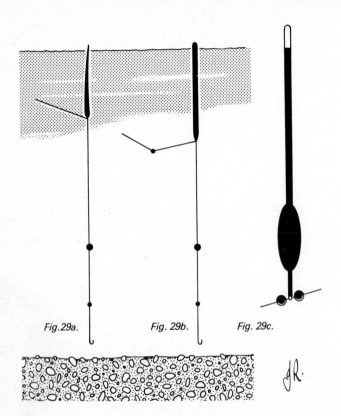

Fig. 29a.   Fig. 29b.   Fig. 29c.

Next we see a straight peacock (Fig 29b). Below the float, the pattern is the same except that we have now added a shot our side of the float, what is called a 'back' shot. This is to speed the sinking of the line beneath the surface to prevent drag caused by the wind interfering with the efficiency of the float. The trick is to cast beyond your baited area, dip the rod tip under the surface of the water and then, by turning the reel, to bring the float over the bait. This not only places the float accurately but sinks the line under the surface. This should be considered standard tactics for *all* still water float fishing. The back shot is usually pinched on 12 ins above the float, further if wind or drag is excessively strong.

Our third still water float is the waggler, a straight peacock with a balsa or cork body at the base (Fig 29c). This, as we said earlier, is there to enable the float to carry more weight. Much of the extra weight in this rig is carried directly under the float in the form of two or even three largish shots, used to lock the float in position on the line at the chosen fishing depth. Below these locked shots, the end pattern is the same as before. Where the straight peacock would take you up to four rod lengths from the bank, this tackle will take you virtually as far as you will ever want to cast, the size of float being scaled up the greater the distance desired.

Special eventualities

Look again at the three float tackles we have just described and you will notice that all three have one important thing in common. In every case, the bait is set to fish *just off* the bottom. While fish often do take a bait offered in this position, there are times when they will do anything but. The first eventuality is when they are taking the bait as it falls down through the water, what anglers call 'on the drop'. How does the shotting pattern change to cope with this eventuality?

The tackle for 'drop' bite fishing

Using a reverse quill for shallow still water fishing as an example (though the same shotting pattern applies whatever loose float you use), a tell-tale shot, the one which will help indicate a bite, is pinched on 18 ins to 2 ft from the hook. All the rest of the shot needed to 'dot' the float are now pinched on directly underneath it. In the example shown (Fig 30a) these are in the 'locked' shot position. The net result of this is that the bait falls much more slowly down through the water, giving fish feeding off the bottom plenty of time to take the bait. This habit of fish taking 'on the drop' is much more likely to occur when you are attempting to induce them to feed by throwing in loose samples of the hookbait or you are using groundbait in its cloud form. Sometimes, an even slower drop than offered by the tackle illustrated is needed. To achieve this, simply move the tell-tale shot nearer the float but never beyond a point that would put it more than halfway up the line between hook and float. 'Drop' bites are signalled by lifting of the float in the water instead of by a submersion.

The second eventuality which must be considered is that the fish turn out to want a still bait on the bottom, in what is called the 'laid on' position. If the fish are shy, they will want the bait on the bottom but *not* the lower shot. (This is shown in Fig 30b.) If they are feeding confidently, however, the shot itself can be laid on. The need for accurate plumbing is never more apparent than when you wish to achieve the position shown in Fig 30b.

Tell-Tale

In using the words 'tell-tale' to describe the lowest shot on the line in shotting patterns, we think it worth a special comment. If a float has been correctly shotted, this is the *only* shot the fish should ever feel. If, therefore, bites are being obtained but fish are not being hooked, it might be presumed that a simple adjustment of the tell-tale shot could help. It's an excellent presumption. It works like this. The shyer the fish are biting, the nearer the tell-tale shot should be moved to the hook although never nearer than 6 ins.

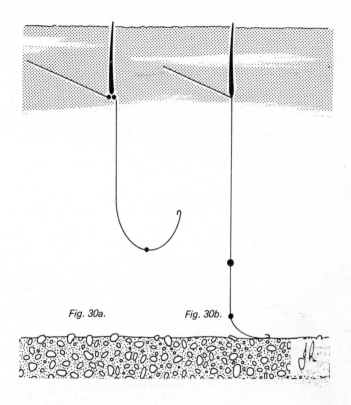

Fig. 30a.

Fig. 30b.

Another yardstick. If the tell-tale is not a dust shot (i.e. the smallest shot), reduce its size for this, too, can make a difference. Small adjustments like these can sometimes make or break your chances of catching fish.

And now

Streamy Water Float Fishing Patterns

While the wind can certainly have nuisance value on any water, its effect is never more critical than when an angler is fishing a river. The big question is simply . . . is the wind blowing upstream or downstream? The answer has absolute bearing on which type of float must be used in this setting, an upstream wind always being easier to cope with than one from the opposite direction. This being the case, let's consider the easier condition first . . .

River Fishing with a Float in an Upstream Wind

When the wind is upstream, the float—whatever its type— should always be fixed to the line at the top and the bottom with a valve rubber. This means that the float is being fished, as anglers say, 'from the top'. In this position, the angler has much greater control of the float than he can ever have in a downstream wind, as we shall see. The impulse of the strike—the act of hooking a fish of which more later—is communicated more directly with this tackle.

Almost without exception in streamy water, the float is cast in and allowed to be carried along by the current, the line it follows through the water being fed with groundbait or loose feed. This method is known as 'trotting' or 'long trotting'.

When trotting with a fixed spool reel, the tackle is cast to a point slightly upstream of the angler's position. Almost immediately, the float will begin moving downstream with the flow. At the same time, the angler lifts his rod to tighten the line between rod top and float (whatever type of float is being used). To allow the float to move easily on downstream, it is necessary to give more line from

the spool before the line tightens so that the float travels downstream smoothly, maintaining the same course. This is done by keeping the bale arm of the reel open and controlling the release of line by putting the index finger on and off the line spool. When a bite occurs, the strike is made against the index finger on the spool, the bale arm being smartly engaged after the fish is hooked. Unless this is carefully done, a small amount of slack line could result and the fish could escape. This is less likely to happen if you are using a closed face reel. The principles are the same . . . except that line is released by pressing and re-pressing the face of the spool, a mechanical aid replacing the work done by the index finger with the fixed spool.

Former World Champion Billy Lane of Coventry initiates a youngster into the art of Avon float fishing on the middle Thames. *(Courtesy: ANS Ltd., Sheffield.)*

There are two ways in which this technique can be used, The first is to let the float run through with the current. The shotting pattern (see Fig 31a) is shown alongside, the float being of the Avon type. One shot is pinched on some 18 ins from the hook. This is the tell-tale and will rarely be bigger than a BB. The rest of the shot needed to 'dot' the float are pinched on about 2 ft above this. This is the classic pattern for fishing a river at the speed of the flow.

But fish do not always want the bait offered in this way. At such times, the answer is often to fish what is known as the string-of-shot system. This is frequently used with a stick float of the type shown in Fig 31b. What happens with this system is that the river is 'trotted' the same way as before, except that the float is checked from time to time by stopping the flow of line from the reel. When this happens, the bait lifts and hovers in an inviting manner and it is at this moment that a bite is most likely. The dotted line in Fig 31b shows what happens when the line is checked. When pinching on shot for the string-of-shot system, start with a small one near the hook—say a No 8 or a No 6—and gradually scale up, making sure that shots between tell-tale and the float are put on equidistant from each other. These, then, are the basic approaches for river fishing with a float in an *upstream* wind. Now . . .

River Fishing with a Float in a Downstream Wind

When this condition exists, the angler's choice is immediately limited and the presentation of the bait can be difficult. The beginner should not shy away from this situation for the time will come when it must be mastered. What happens now is that the float must *always* be fixed 'bottom only' (to enable the line to be buried beneath the surface out of the way of the wind) and the tackle must *always* be fished at the speed of the current (to check a loose float in a river is to submerge it thus registering a false bite). The line is buried out of the way of the wind to enable the angler to retain sufficient control. This ensures that the bait precedes the

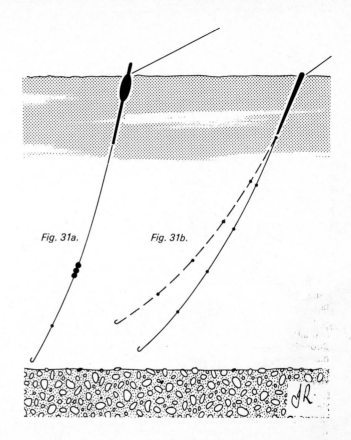

Fig. 31a.   Fig. 31b.

float as it moves down the swim. The float most used for this eventuality (though there are others) is the Waggler, a peacock quill with a balsa or cork body at the base. The diagram (Fig 32) shows the shotting with a Waggler . . . below the float the classic Avon pattern but, because of the 'bottom only' fitting, the line is buried. In extreme conditions a back shot can be introduced (as in Fig 29b) to speed this process.

Some working tips when float fishing rivers

Always when trotting, try to keep as much of the line as possible off the water. Do this by holding the rod up. In a downstream wind, the aim, and you won't always succeed, is to have the line reasonably tight between rod tip and the base of the float or, if one is being employed, the back shot.

When baiting, remember that the stronger the current the further the bait must be thrown in upstream of the point at which you are fishing to ensure that it reaches bottom in the area being fished. Loose feed is good in rivers, but, if the current is strong, it will be necessary to use groundbait to get samples of the hookbait down to the fish.

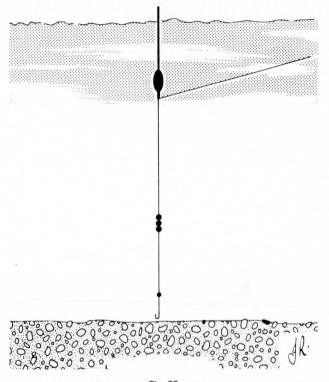

Fig. 32.

And now

LEGERING

First let's deal with technique for still waters and sluggish rivers. In this setting, the best approach for the beginner is with a swing tip. How this is fitted was described earlier. The end tackle should be the fixed paternoster also shown earlier (Fig 22).

Always, when swing tipping, set up shop so that you are fishing with your back to the wind. Always use two rod rests, one to support the rod near the tip, the other at the butt. Position these so that when the rod is in the rests, it is pointing down wind, i.e. if the wind is from left to right, the rod will be fished to the right.

After the cast, the tip will be held in a horizontal direction as the Arlesey bomb (Fig 21) is falling through the water. As soon as it hits bottom, the tip will begin to fall back. That's when the rod is placed in the rests and the line tightened to the bomb until, eventually, the tip is hanging just off vertical with the line tight between bomb and tip. Bites will now be signalled by a forward or backward movement of the tip (Fig 33a). More complex methods can be used with the swing tip—like fishing for 'drop' bites—but these are best left until you have ceased to be a beginner.

When legering in a flowing river, the best thing to try first is the quiver tip (Fig 33b). Fit this to the screw in end ring of the rod and again make up the fixed paternoster rig at the end of the line. Cast downstream and out and let the bomb roll round with the current. Most bites will come once the bomb has stopped. At that moment, the rod should be placed in a rest so that the rod is pointing straight to your front. Sometimes bites will occur when the bomb is still moving. Keep an eye on the tip during this movement and strike at any dramatic movement of the tip, or if anything happens which releases the tension on it. The same kind of signals—a forward movement or pronounced slackening of

pressure on the tip—are obtained when the bait is stationary. Don't forget that the quiver tip can also be useful in strong winds on still water. When fishing in this circumstance, the rod should be set up so that it is being fished parallel with the bank.

If you haven't got a quiver tip—or if the current is too strong for a quiver tip—the answer in a river is rod top legering. The method is the same as that described for quiver tipping, except that bites are signalled by the tip of the rod itself. Due to the greater stiffness of the rod tip as opposed to a quiver tip, the amount of movement tends to be not so great.

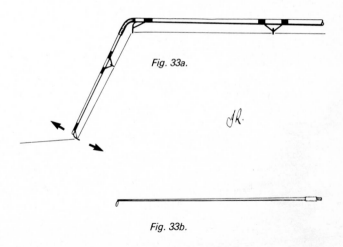

Fig. 33a.

Fig. 33b.

Legering tips

The most important tip is to try always to place your groundbait and your hookbait in the same place. When swingtipping, the best dodge is to cast beyond the bait so that when the line is tightened the bait will be drawn onto the groundbait. A useful still water technique where the bed is free of obstructions is called the 'twitch'. After the bait has settled, leave it for a few minutes. If no bite has resulted, lift the rod about six inches from the rest and move it about 12 ins to right or left (whichever is appropriate) being careful to keep the swingtip properly 'cocked'. Now bring the tip back to the rest, taking up the small amount of slack line created by turning the reel. A bite during the 'twitch' movement will be dramatically signalled but, mostly, the bite will occur a split second after the rod has been returned to the rest. It follows that if the first 'twitch' doesn't produce a bite, the process should be repeated at intervals of about a minute. If no fish are encountered, the bait is re-cast and the process repeated. Remember, it is usually far better to move a bait by 'twitching' it with a swing tip than to let it lie dormant in the hope that it will be found by the fish. If the bed of the river is very dirty you may have no alternative but to fish a still bait.

Now so far, we have talked about the mechanics of making contact with a fish. What happens once you have got a bite? The first thing is . . .

The Strike

This is the name given to the movement of the rod used to secure the hook in the fish's mouth. Almost without exception, beginners strike too hard. Generally the strike is a smart upward movement of the rod . . . though in shallow water, it's better to make a sideways strike. Don't wallop the fish. Imagine you are lifting the bait into the fish's mouth and that you are not trying to break its jaw and you'll soon get the idea. The greater the distance at which you are fishing, the more force you must use, *not* to set the hook but to tighten the greater amount of line lying between you and the fish. Before fishing, make certain that the slipping clutch on your reel has been set so that it will give line if a fish likely to tax the line strength being used takes the bait. In our view, the slipping clutch is at its most useful as an aid when striking.

Playing the fish

Once hooked, it is important that the fish is moved as quickly as possible from the spot where it was hooked so as not to let it disturb the rest of the shoal and that the line between rod and fish be kept tight. This is done by keeping the rod top held up. If you give a fish any slack line while playing it, it can easily escape from the hook. If the fish is not large, it will be found that it can be reeled in with little or no difficulty. If it is big then it may be necessary to give it line during the fight. Some do this by means of the slipping clutch but we prefer to do it by letting the fish take line with the finger used as a brake on the back of the reel spool or, if it's possible, by back winding. With a fish like this, it's equally certain that you will have to 'pump' it in. The rod is lifted and the fish comes towards you. As the rod is lowered, line is gained by turning the reel until you are ready to lift again and lower again. This is what we call 'pumping'. Another problem arises if the fish heads for a weedbed. To try and stop it dead in its tracks, especially if it's a powerful fish, could lead to a break. The answer, if the fish does make it to the weed, is not to try and drag it out by brute force. First of all, let the line go slack. The reduction of pressure often persuades the fish to swim clear of its own accord. If this doesn't happen, apply *gentle* pressure in an effort to retain just the right amount of contact as you guide the fish through the weed. Once the fish is near the bank you are ready for . . .

Netting the fish

Probably more fish are lost at the net than anywhere else and, in most cases, it's because the net was not properly positioned *before* the fish was hooked. Wherever possible, always have the landing net already *in the water*. Then, when the fish is within netting range, the net can be *gently* brought up to scoop it out. Never try and net a fish too soon. Ideally, the fish should be lying spent on the surface before the net is used. Always remember you are bringing the fish to the net and not the net to the fish. Remember, too, that any sudden movement can produce a rapid reaction from the fish which could permit it to get free. Once netted the next job is . . .

Unhooking the fish

If the fish has been correctly hooked in the jaw, unhooking is easy. Simply take the shank of the hook between thumb and forefinger. Give a gentle but firm twist and it should be out. If the fish has taken the hook into its mouth or throat, the disgorger must be used. The method of its removal will depend on the type of disgorger you bought. When using a disgorger, always keep the line to the hook tight—and be gentle. This way you will most certainly remove the hook with the minimum discomfort to the fish. And, talking of comfort, brings us to our final point . . .

Caring for your fish

As every reader should be aware, coarse fishermen keep their fish in a net—called, not surprisingly, a keepnet—so that they can be released alive at the end of the day to fight another time. Fish can die in keepnets that are too small. If your pocket permits, never use a net less than 6 ft long or 18 ins in diameter. If possible, use the new knotless type as these protect the fish even more. Always make sure that as much of the net as possible is submerged and, in shallow water, try to peg it so that it is fully extended. The more freedom you give the fish in the net the better they'll like it.

When returning fish, don't simply tip the net up and drop them back into the water. Tip it gently and ease the fish into the water. Make sure that all have swum safely away. Some may lie on their sides because of the shock. Right them and hold them in that position until they're ready to swim away.

Pleased with his catch, this angler is equally careful to see that the fish which delighted him is safely returned alive to the water *(Courtesy: ANS Ltd., Sheffield.)*

PIKE FISHING

Pike are one of the most popular species with beginners. They can be very big fish . . . which makes them an exciting prospect on the end of a line. They are widely distributed around the country, but there are more of them in shallow, slow or still water fisheries—which helps make them quite easy to catch.

The pike is a predator—which means that it feeds mainly on living and dead fish but sometimes even on animals and birds. So, to catch a pike, you need to offer a live or dead fish, or an imitation fish in a manner which gives the pike the opportunity to grab it.

It follows that, if you are a beginner to coarse fishing, you may have difficulty catching fish to use as livebait, and lots of time can be wasted if six or more dace, small roach or rudd are not available to you quickly.

Which leaves two alternatives, either fish with a deadbait bought from the fishmonger—like herring, mackerel or sprats—or use artificial baits. Many of the biggest pike caught every season are taken on deadbait, so there is ample proof that sea fish are good for deadbait fishing. Many expert anglers think they are better!

Spinning for pike is perhaps the easiest. Once you have purchased a small number of lures you can go pike fishing whenever the fancy takes you without having first to obtain bait of any kind. This is the method which produces the greatest number of pike, except perhaps in the colder parts of the winter. While the water is relatively warm, pike will chase fish—or imitation fish—with enthusiasm, but when the water becomes cold pike are less active and less inclined to swim after a moving bait. That's when they are more likely to take an anchored live or deadbait.

The disadvantage many expert pike fishermen see in spinning is that it takes many small pike for every big one . . . but that is an advantage for a beginner. Better to acquire experience by catching small to medium size pike first so that when that first big pike comes along it can be landed and played with expertise.

Tackle for spinning (Fig 34): a 9 ft to 10 ft glass or cane rod, fixed-spool reel, 10 lbs to 12 lbs breaking strain monofilament line (with the reel's spool filled to one-eighth of an inch of its rim), three 3 ft wire traces, fitted with a swivel at one end and a link swivel at the other, and an assortment of not less than four spoons or other lures.

You will also need anti-kink leads and spiral leads—which help you to cast a light lure a good distance—and a spacious landing net. In addition, you need an instrument called a gag to help you open your pike's mouth once you have landed it and a long-handled disgorger to remove the hooks (Fig 35).

As with floats, most tackle shops offer a wide variety of spoons and other lures for sale. Play safe. Buy medium size rather than small or big ones. Baits measuring from 2½ ins to 4 ins long will catch any pike that swims . . . on the right day. Lures coloured partially red can be good, with brass or gold coloured baits also good.

The spoon or lure is attached to the link swivel on the wire trace you will also have bought and your reel line is fastened to the plain swivel at the upper end of the trace with a tucked half blood knot (Fig 19). The anti-kink lead may not be necessary; much depends on the efficiency of the swivels in the trace, but if the line accumulates turns and kinks and it starts to tangle, then an anti-kink lead is very necessary.

The casting technique for spinning is much the same as for bottom fishing for roach or bream. Cast across the water, allow time—though not too much—for the lure to sink to the required depth and then retrieve slowly. Raise and lower and twitch the rod

Fig. 34.

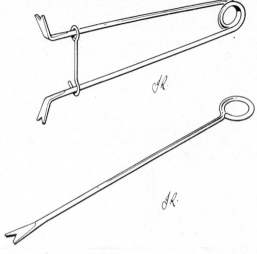

Fig. 35.

Fig 34: Tackle used for pike spinning.
At the top, a wire trace with a barrel swivel on one end and on the other a link swivel to which the spinner (or plug) is attached. In the centre left is an anti-kink lead and on the right, a spiral lead. On the left at the bottom, is a Colorado spoon. This type is fixed at both ends and revolves round a central spindle. On the right (bottom) is a kidney spoon with a blade attached at the top only. The advantage of the latter is that it can be retrieved at slower speeds than the Colorado type.

top during the retrieve to help convince the pike that your lure is an injured fish it is capable of catching with ease. Ideally, a spoon bait—or any other metal lure—should be fished 12 ins to 3 ft off the bottom. The clutch on the fixed spool reel should be adjusted so that a big fish can take line from the spool even while you are reeling in. This prevents the line from snapping and also ensures that the rod is not subject to more strain than it can handle.

Plug Fishing

Plugs, like spoons, are imitation fish (Fig 36). They are designed to perform all sorts of tricks in the water. Some can float and are used for surface fishing in quite shallow water. Others are fitted with diving vane (see Fig 36 again) which makes them move up and down when they are retrieved. Plugs are generally more buoyant than spoons which means they can be retrieved much more slowly and this can be sometimes crucial when there are half interested pike around.

Deadbait Fishing

For this purpose, you need a 10 ft to 12 ft rod, a fixed spool reel (loaded with 10 to 12 lbs breaking strain line), and some Jardine snap tackles (see Fig 38a).

The most used method is simply to leger the bait which may be a herring, a sprat or, currently fashionable, half a mackerel. In Fig 37, you will see two end rigs. If any distance is to be cast, the two hook rig is the best. The two hooks on the Jardine snap are secured on the fish's flank as shown and the trace is then threaded with a baiting needle through the fish's body and out at the tail (shown by dotted lines in the diagram). The single hook tackle is self-explanatory.

All you need do then is attach the loop of your wire trace to the reel line by means of a swivel and cast out, watching the line for the kind of movement which spells a take.

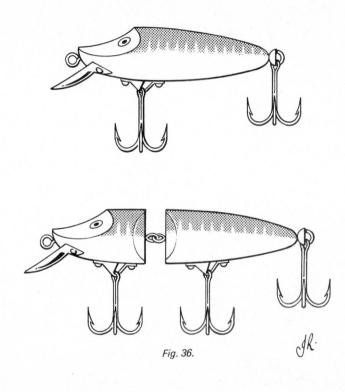

Fig. 36.

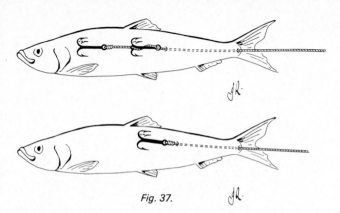

Fig. 37.

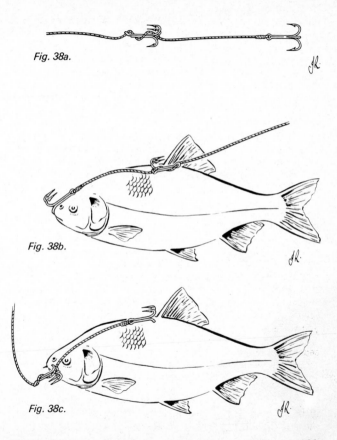

Fig. 38a.

Fig. 38b.

Fig. 38c.

Livebait Fishing

The same rod suggested for deadbaiting will serve for live-baiting, too. The problem with filling the reel with monofilament for this technique is that this tends to sink below the surface between rod and float. This makes it difficult to strike cleanly and to play the pike after it is hooked. The answer is to use braided terylene line. This should be lightly greased by winding it onto the reel through a rag impregnated with line floatant. It will then give no trouble.

The Jardine snap tackle (Fig 38a) is the best end tackle for beginners to use. This consists of two treble hooks, the lower one fixed, the upper one movable on a length of wire to enable the tackle to accommodate different sizes of livebait.

There are two basic ways of setting the snap tackle on the livebait. In still or sluggish water, the system shown in Fig 38b is best. In running water, i.e. a river, the second method (Fig 38c) is to be preferred.

Fig. 39 shows the complete livebait tackle. The trace (i.e. the Jardine snap) has been connected via a barrel swivel to a float of the Fishing Gazette type.

When using this tackle the cast should be made smoothly to ensure that the bait is not thrown from the hooks. This can happen! Better to cast only 10 to 20 yds and keep your bait on than to attempt greater distances only to cast the bait away. Better still, if conditions and the liveliness of the bait permits, to have it swim out of its own accord after being gently lowered into the water.

It often pays to cast towards reedbeds, weedbeds, or over-hanging trees for pike can be more numerous near cover. Make use of the wind by casting across the direction from which it is blowing. This in turn affects the float and the livebait will swim over a bigger area than when it is cast down wind.

When a pike takes the bait the float will disappear and the line usually begins to tighten. If necessary, allow the pike to take line by giving it more before you actually draw the hooks home into the fish. Count up to 10 before striking and you are likely to hook the fish but delay any longer and the hooks are likely to be deep down inside the pike's throat and you don't want that.

When a pike takes a bait it always grabs it sideways. After a pause, the pike then 'turns' the bait in its mouth and then—and only then—swallows it. This means that if you strike too soon you simply pull the bait—and the hooks—out of the pike's jaws.

Points to remember: The pike fishing season varies throughout the country. It is safe to assume you can fish for pike anywhere from October 1 to March 14, but in some areas livebait is banned in the summer. You will need a can to contain your livebait. Remember to change the water in the can regularly or the fish will die through lack of oxygen.

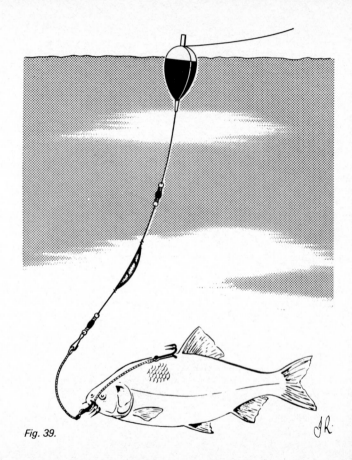

Fig. 39.

CARP FISHING

The number of anglers who specialise in carp is very small compared to those who prefer roach, bream or pike, but everyone admits that the carp is a powerful and attractive fish to catch. Once hooked, it often dives away strongly and the angler has a great fight on his hands. This is part of the fish's appeal, but it is anything but easy to catch. Most carp anglers are highly delighted if they can average one carp every time they fish.

Most carp are found in still water lakes, rarely in rivers. They prefer the water temperature at summer level, with the result that they are not often caught in winter. Certainly no beginner should start by carp fishing in winter or he will soon rate fishing an unrewarding pastime!

Carp tackle is stronger than that used for roach and bream. It has to be. Carp are sometimes caught on small hooks and frail lines, but the beginner should err on the heavy side with his tackle.

He needs a 10½ ft to 12 ft comparatively stiff hollowglass or cane rod, fixed-spool reel, 10 lbs breaking strain line and hooks sized from 8 to 2. All other requirements are identical with those for other forms of freshwater fishing.

Carp are shy fish and for that reason are more regularly caught either after dark or early and late in the day. That's not to say that carp cannot be caught during the day. They can, but much depends on the colour of the water, the sunshine, wind, temperature and other factors.

A carp fishing beginner would do well to ask more questions of his local tackle dealer than he would if after roach or bream. Carp inhabit relatively few waters so the first essential is to establish whether or not the fish are present in the water you have in mind.

Late-evening fishing is perhaps best for beginners. Plan to arrive at the waterside to fish the last three hours of daylight and, if you are keen, to continue after dark.

Two carp anglers wait patiently for a bite. Notice the camouflage screen they have erected to hide themselves from the fish. *(Courtesy: National Benzole Co. Ltd.)*

41

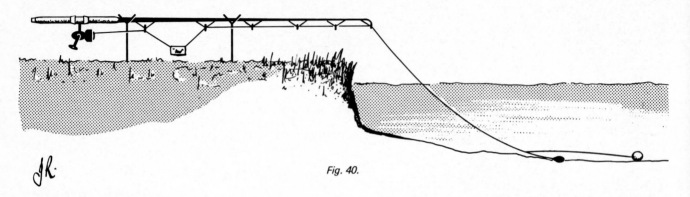

Fig. 40.

Carp fishing has less technical complications than all other sorts of fishing. The hook is tied direct to the reel line, with a paternoster-fished Arlesey bomb or shot leger providing the casting weight where this is necessary. (See Fig 22.)

Bread in one form or another is the best all-round hookbait. It can be used as bread flake, or as paste, or even crust, the latter having the advantage of being rather easier to keep on the hook during casting.

Carp specialists use leger tactics almost exclusively, though float fishing is used to catch smaller carp like crucians.

The hook is baited with a biggish piece of bread—as big as a 50p piece if 10 lbs-plus fish are the target. The bait is cast out and allowed to sink to the bottom. The line is then tightened and the rod laid into two rod rests.

The spool of the reel is left open, with the bale arm disengaged. A small piece of silver paper can be folded over the line between the lower rod rings, or between the butt ring and the reel, and this becomes the bite indicator. When a carp bites, the silver paper moves upwards, the line tightens and more is taken from the spool (see Fig 40).

Once the run has developed and line is moving away nicely, then set the hook gently . . . and the fun begins. The carp will run hard for whatever cover exists close at hand, and if this is a dense weedbed, for example, the angler must do his best to prevent the fish diving into it. The clutch of the reel must be finely set to ensure that the maximum pressure the rod can give is applied before the clutch slips and concedes line to the fish.

Other baits for carp: worms, maggots, cheese, cheese paste, pet food pastes, and potato.